I0794135

FUN with FOOD WEBS

TROPICAL RAINFOREST FOOD WEBS

Written by Charis Mather

KidHaven PUBLISHING

Published in 2024 by
KidHaven Publishing, an Imprint of Greenhaven Publishing, LLC
2544 Clinton St., Buffalo, NY 14224

Written by: Charis Mather
Edited by: Rebecca Phillips-Bartlett
Designed by: Dan Scase

Image Credits
All images are courtesy of Shutterstock.com, unless otherwise specified—with thanks to Getty Images, Thinkstock Photo, and iStockphoto. Cover – Ondrej Prosicky, Papamoon, Murilo Mazzo, Leonardo Mercon, accarvalhophotography, Teo Tarras, Thananun Leungchaiya. 4–5 – Pete Niesen, Dinael Oropeza. 6–7 – Trismegist san. 8–9 – BorneoRimbawan, Ammit Jack. 10–11 – imageBROKER.com, Shahedul Sifat, Orenn. 12–13 – EsHanPhot, Conservationist, Pete Niesen, Nacho Such. 14–15 –Thorsten Spoerlein, Daniel Dorantes. 16–17 – Petr Salinger, Ondrej Prosicky. 18–19 – Vinicius R. Souza, Mark_Kostich. 20–21 – feathercollector, Dmitrii Kash. 22–23 – kentoh, Ondrej Prosicky, Dmitrii Kash, Pete Niesen, Mark_Kostich, Daniel Dorantes, Nacho Such, Ondrej Prosicky, Shahedul Sifat, Orenn.

Cataloging-in-Publication Data

Names: Mather, Charis, 1999-.
Title: Tropical rainforest food webs / Charis Mather.
Description: Buffalo, New York: KidHaven Publishing, 2024. |
Series: Fun with food webs | Includes glossary and index.
Identifiers: ISBN 9781534546110 (pbk.) | ISBN 9781534546127 (library bound) |
ISBN 9781534546134 (ebook)
Subjects: LCSH: Rain forest ecology--Amazon River Region--Juvenile literature. |
Food chains (Ecology)--Amazon River Region--Juvenile literature.
Classification: LCC QH112.M38 2024 | DDC 577.340981'1--dc23

Manufactured in the United States of America

CPSIA compliance information: Batch #CW24KH: For further information contact Greenhaven Publishing LLC at 1-844-317-7404.

Please visit our website, www.greenhavenpublishing.com.
For a free color catalog of all our high-quality books, call toll free 1-844-317-7404 or fax 1-844-317-7405.

Find us on

CONTENTS

Words that look like ***THIS*** can be found in the glossary on page 24.

THE TROPICAL RAINFOREST ECOSYSTEM

From the very tops of the trees down to the forest floor, tropical rainforests are full of life. These warm, wet ***HABITATS*** make perfect homes for millions of different types of plants and animals.

Every living thing in the rainforest needs food. Sometimes, that means eating other living things. **PREDATORS**, **PREY**, and plants are all important parts of the tropical rainforest **ECOSYSTEM**.

Food Chains and Food Webs

A food chain is a helpful way to see the order in which living things are eaten. Things that are eaten first are at the bottom. Creatures that eat others are higher up.

a tropical rainforest food chain

Most living things are part of more than one food chain. When multiple food chains connect in different places, they make a food web.

PRODUCERS

The bottom of a food web is made up of producers. These are living things that can make their own food instead of getting **ENERGY** by eating other things. Many producers use sunlight to do this.

The most common types of producers are plants.

When producers get eaten by other living things, some of the energy in them moves up the chain. Creatures who eat producers need to eat a lot of them to get enough energy.

Banyan Trees

Food: made with energy from the sun

Eaten by: scarlet macaws, toucans, monkeys, sloths, bats

There are millions of producers in tropical rainforests. One of these producers is the banyan tree. Banyan trees grow figs. These fruits are eaten by many animals living up in the trees.

Bromeliads

Many animals in the rainforest eat the leaves and colorful flowers of bromeliad plants. Some bromeliads have leaves that are shaped in a way that collects water for small animals to live in.

Food:	Eaten by:
made with energy from the sun	monkeys, sloths, scarlet macaws, bats

CONSUMERS

Consumers are the next step above producers in a food web. They eat other living things. Consumers that only eat plants are herbivores. Consumers that eat meat are carnivores. Omnivores eat both plants and meat.

Sloths

Food:
leaves, twigs, flowers, fruit

Eaten by:
jaguars, harpy eagles, anacondas, ocelots

Sloths live in the rainforest's ***canopy***. Some sloths spend lots of time hanging upside down. They do not often leave the canopy, because it is safer for them to stay up in the trees where there is also plenty of food for them to eat.

Scarlet Macaws

Scarlet macaws are large, brightly colored parrots. They live in the trees at the very top of the rainforest. Sometimes, scarlet macaws make their homes inside tree trunks where predators cannot see them.

Food:	Eaten by:
fruit, seeds, nuts, flowers, leaves, insects, snails	anacondas, harpy eagles, some monkeys, hawks

Scarlet macaws have large beaks that help them crack open seeds and nuts. These birds do not just eat plants, though. They eat insects and snails too.

White-Faced Capuchin Monkeys

White-faced capuchin monkeys are omnivores. They eat fruit, leaves, nuts, and other plants that they find in the treetops. These clever animals sometimes use tools such as rocks to help them get their food.

Food:	Eaten by:
baby scarlet macaws, bromeliads, fruit, seeds, nuts, leaves, frogs	jaguars, harpy eagles, snakes, hawks

Other than plants, these monkeys also eat frogs and small birds. Sometimes, they will eat young scarlet macaws and eggs that they find in nests.

Apex Predators

The top of a food web is made up of apex predators. These are consumers that hunt other animals for food but are not hunted themselves.

Green Anacondas

Food:	Eaten by:
large **rodents**, birds, tapirs, sloths, deer, sheep	no one

Green anacondas catch prey with their strong jaws, then squeeze them with their bodies. They swallow their meals whole, even if their prey is much larger than they are.

Harpy Eagles

The rainforest canopy is also home to harpy eagles. These large apex predators are as scary as they look. Their long claws are excellent at snatching up prey—even prey as large as deer!

Harpy eagles ***PERCH*** high up in the trees while they look for prey. They have excellent eyesight, which helps them spot animals in the thick forests. Then, they swoop down to grab their meal.

Food:
capuchin monkeys, sloths, scarlet macaws, opossums, deer

Eaten by:
no one

A TROPICAL RAINFOREST FOOD WEB

Look at this food web! It shows how energy moves through the tropical rainforest ecosystem. Start with the sun and producers at the bottom, and follow the arrows to see what gets eaten by what.

How many producers can you see on this food web?

GLOSSARY

canopy the uppermost spreading, branchy layer of a forest

ecosystem a community of living things and the area they live in

energy the power and ability to do work

habitats the natural homes for animals, plants, and other living things

perch to rest on something

predators animals that hunt other animals for food

prey animals that are hunted by other animals for food

rodents mammals, such as mice, rats, and squirrels, that have long front teeth that grow throughout their whole lives

INDEX